This is a self help book for

SME Entrepreneurs

Dedicated to my Parents

Shri R. B. Jaiswal

And

Smt. Urmila Devi

Preface

It's the first day of the lockdown due to COVID - 19 pandemic, when I am starting to begin my this long pending project. Today I have grown with working experience of 19 years and 10 months. My career path has not been an impressive one in terms of the organizations I have worked for. When people ask, which companies you have worked with, my generic answer is "*You may not know these companies by name as I have always worked with the smaller companies but have contributed well in their growth.*" And I feel proud saying so.

Yes, I have always worked with SMEs or start ups. But I have no grudge in saying so as I find that my learning curve has been far better than those of my friends and batch mates who have been working with blue chip multinational companies.

I know the nerve of SMEs. Working with so many of them, I can read the pulse of any SME. The saga is that most of the SME owners do not work with a vision. They remain money centric and live with fears and stigmas in life. I actually remain surprised that being an entrepreneur, a SME owner remains under stress of losing their data and information, which are easily available to anyone in today's world of fast changing technologies. They refrain from outsourcing or hiring consultants for this very reason and tend to ignore the facts that internal employees handling their data and information can very easily be hired by a competitor. This is also a fact. Any new entrant in any industry hires the entire team of its competitor and takes charge of their large segment of market share in very less time.

Another fact that I have noticed is that SME owners take their business as their hobby. They want to do everything on their own. They will involve themselves in all aspects of business as if only they can do those jobs and it's very hard to break this myth. In my career I have found many, who were very harsh, when I tried to point this as their lacuna.

However, there are also SME owners, who are visionary and broadminded. Only people from this category create history and become giant corporations, because they focus on doing only jobs which they are expert in. It's a very big myth today that by using Google one can do anything, ignoring the fact that Google does not provide any solution; it just directs you to an expert's page who is expert in solving that particular problem.

This book is meant for such visionary entrepreneurs only. My objective of writing this book is to make SMEs aware of the secrets of growing big. And the secret is that; let your systems run your business not your people. As many consultants truly say *"Work on your business and not in your business"*.

In this book I will try to touch upon the areas which are required to be focused on to systemize a business so that as a business owner, you remain free to focus only on the business development activities. If implemented well, spending one day in operational and execution areas of business shall be sufficient enough.

Chapters

Chapter 1: Systems and Processes

Chapter 2: It's Perpetual

Chapter 3: Organization Structure

Chapter 4: Templates and Formats

Chapter 5: Work Procedures

Chapter 6: Control Mechanisms

Chapter 7: Systems and Processes Vs Automation

Chapter 8: Building a Team

Chapter 9: Focus on Marketing & Sales

Chapter 1: Systems and Processes

Systems are like policies and Processes are like procedures, if one understands the difference between them.

Google defines it as:

"A system is the overall "thing", or a core element, you're looking to have and/ or implement in your business. It's something that helps your business run. The processes are all the things you do in order to make any given system work most efficiently."

Systems are the ways to do the things to attain the desired results. In a business the end result is profit and the only thumb rule to increase the profit is to increase the gap between revenue and cost. Therefore giving importance to creating systems for increasing revenue and reducing the products or services cost and overhead costs, is a very important task of a business owner.

Some examples of a system in any organization can be as below:

- Customer order shall not be taken into processing unless advance payment is credited in the company's account.
- Sales team to obtain approval from MD for extending more than 20% discount to the customers.
- Immediately after the dispatch an email to customer shall be send with detailed dispatch and tracking details
- For any purchase in the company, a PO shall be issued by the competent authority in the company.
- The Accounts Team will not initiate any payment unless a bill is entered in books of accounts.
- Conveyance bills shall be passed by reporting authority before submitting to accounts for payment.

- Any employee to send an application for leave in 3 days advance for any casual leave up to 2 days.
- Production to start only after a Job Card is issued by the PPC department.

Similarly, entire organization can be systemized in a manner that one does not need to apply their minds to get any work done. Approvals, escalations, controls, exclusions, appraisals etc. can be done through such systems. The more systems for everything we create, more independent the organization becomes from people. It is seen that companies with no or least systems are more dependent on people and always stress more upon retaining people over business development.

Every entrepreneur must have a deep understanding of these systems. Unless one understands the importance of it and firmly decides to implement this, running business on autopilot may just become a daydream.Having understood the systems we should try to understand the process now. What are processes? Process is the step by step guide to implement any system. To make the audience understand this I will again illustrate an example. It's an exercise

Take a blank paper and draw a rose with your imagination...

DONE??

Now, read below instructions and draw a rose following these instructions:

1. Start your rose drawing, by drawing an oval shape.

2. **Draw a small spiral inside the oval.**

3. **Draw a heart around the spiral**

4. **Draw a line following both sides of the heart shape**

5. **Now draw a U shape**

6. **Draw a curved line from the tip of the V to the bottom**

   of the blossom.

7. **Draw a few sepals under the flower.**

8. **Draw the stem and a leaf.**

Now observe the difference. When people draw rose with their imagination,

No, drawing will be the same. It will rather be weird. While anyone drawing a rose with the above set of instructions will draw the same rose every time. The given sets of instructions are nothing but process. Processes are generally termed as workflows or SOPs in organizations.

Before summing up this chapter, I would like to give an example of McDonalds.

There are thousands of outlets of McDonald's throughout India, and if you walk in any of these outlets and order for a McVeggie burger, you will get the same burger at every counter. You will not be able to distinguish between these in any manner be it size, cutlet, taste or anything. How is it made possible? While you will see that staff working at these counters is young boys and girls and their average job life cycle at McDonalds would not be more than a year.

It's all about Systems and Processes that are running this one of the largest chains of the world.

Co-relating with this example you can visualize many companies around us which are being driven by Systems and not by people.

We would often hear that big fortune 500 companies remove their CXOs for one reason or another overnight. Why are they not afraid of removing them? Because those companies are running on Systems.

On the contrary our SME owner is always under fear of losing even its accountants, forget about CXOs. I have often heard entrepreneurs saying that we don't get good people these days. Whereas the fact remains that you would not be required to hunt for **"THE RIGHT PEOPLE"**, if you have strong Systems and Processes.

I understand that by now, the reader of this book has understood the meaning and relevance of Systems and Processes. Here it is a must to mention that a pilot switches on the **"AUTOPILOT"** in his/ her plane, only after the plane has settled in the sky and is running smoothly. Before that he/ she has to do all activities to take off the plane safely and set off all the operations.

So, my friend, one needs to first set up strong systems and processes in his organization before, he go on **"AUTOPILOT"**.

Chapter 2: Its Perpetual

I often get a query from entrepreneurs that, how long will it take to set our systems?

Every time when I am asked this question, I simply say that it's not a onetime activity. Yes, every company creates some systems, since inception itself. No company runs without systems; however the effectiveness of systems may not be up to the mark to scale it. Or at times the organization head may not have the right kind of exposure to create the robust systems, before they started or joined this business. This is the very reason that after reaching a certain level, the man on the top, remains busy in operational activities and thereby growth of the company becomes stagnant.

The major role of the CXOs in the organizations remains to work on systems and processes to suit the strategies. With any change in the strategy related to marketing, sales, product offerings, customer services or any other thing in the organization, systems need to be reworked. Its perpetual in nature.

While small changes in the systems keep happening in the companies, it must re-engineer the entire systems and processes of the company in a holistic manner after a given time period. This period precisely varies between 2-3 years, but it is vital for the organization's continuous growth. Some systems need changes immediately after change in government policies. Any sudden change in statutory compliances may require sudden relook and change of systems.

Large organizations hire a separate team to continuously work on systems and processes, which may not be practical for SMEs. However, fact remains that at every level of growth systems need to be revamped. Indicators of relooking into the systems again and to rework those, is when the owner's involvement starts increasing in the business operations to keep the things in order i.e. he starts to get involved again in the problem solving and fire fighting.

So the conclusion is that once the plane is in *AUTOPILOT* mode, it cannot be in *AUTOPILOT* forever. Systems & Processes need continuous changes and improvements.

A business should assess its current situation and business scenario and should work to create a robust system as per current scenario, with an objective to let business run without his/ her more involvement and then keep an eye on that for further improvement to ensure rapid and continuous growth. Here, I would like to give an example that the company I got involved with as a consultant seven years ago, when they were just a start up, is still in my clientele list and I am constantly working on their systems for improvement and to suit their changing business strategies. Today in just seven years this company has created a remarkable footprint in the industry they work in.

Now, when our reader has understood the relevance of systems and processes, let me take him/ her towards the *how* part of the game. In proceeding chapters, I will explain how one can set up strong systems and processes of his/ her own organization.

Chapter 3: Organization Structure

Entire organization's processes consist of different sets of activities. To perform each activity a separate set of knowledge and expertise is required. Therefore, we create a bundle of activities which require a particular subject's knowledge and expertise. We call such bundles as sanctions in the organizations. For every function a different team is required and team size may vary based on the work load or amount of business being done by the company. However, it may sometimes not be related to the quantum of business being done in the company in terms of money. Team size is directly proportional to the number of transactions being done in the organization and not based on the value of the transactions.

As a promoter of business, an entrepreneur must know the number of people required to handle the number of transactions for any particular task. This will be the basis for judging the size of organization in terms of manpower. Therefore, it becomes important for any business to create a crystal clear organization structure.

Now, to create an organization structure, which is aligned with the business goals, one must have a clear understanding of the goals. An organization structure must be created based on the goal where a businessman wants to achieve. One should not look at the current strength of the organization while doing so. At the same time one may keep the current team out of the mind while preparing the organization structure. One must visualize an organization which is required to reach to the desired level. Keep the manpower budget, competence level and manpower turnover related issues out of the mind while defining the organization chart.

Once again, give a good and quality time in visualizing the dream team and the hierarchy structure, which will take you to the desired level. Prepare this structure on a piece of paper and name every position along with the function. While doing so do not care about the designations given to the staff. Like a Supply Chain Head may be later designated as VP/ Director/ GM/ Manager or whatever but the role that he/ she is playing is of SCM head. Similarly the team reporting to SCM head may be designated whatever later but it can be named middle level or junior level or entry level position while preparing the organization chart. Also, while preparing this structure please visualize and define the layers in the structure. For an effective management of people and work, not more than three people should be reporting to any position in the organization. This is applicable for any position, even for the head of the organization.

Once a clear organization structure is created, come the task of jotting down the roles of every position created in the structure. Roles are defined based on the processes required for implementing any system. This can be well understood with an example. Like if there is a system defined in any organization that says *"The Accounts team will not initiate any payment unless a bill is entered in the books of accounts."* Now the process to implement this system can be..

1- All purchase bills to be obtained from the vendors by the purchase department.

2- Purchase bills to be approved by the competent authority.

3- After approval the purchase department will hand over the bill to the accounts department and will keep a record of this handover.

4- The Accounts team will enter the bill in the books of accounts being maintained in tally (or whatever accounting software being used).

5- The Account team will maintain a real time list of creditors.

6- Accounts team will obtain approval from finance team for fund availability and allocation to the creditors.

7- The Accounts team will prepare the cheque / initiate the payment to the creditors.

Now in the above seven steps process of a system, the role of Purchase Team, Accounts Team and Finance Team is inherited. However, this role of these teams is not limited to this only system. Their roles will be derived from the processes against multiple systems in the organization. Using the above methodology, one can create the role of every position defined in the organization structure.

Next step would be to define the Key Result Areas of every position in the organization structure. KRAs are nothing but to define the measurable points against the role of the position. Like one of the KRA for Purchase Team can be to submit the vendor bill in accounts, after all due approvals, within 3 days of the goods or services are received / availed by the company. Defining roles is an incomplete activity if the KRAs are not defined against every position.

Once KRAs are defined, the reporting from every position should be defined. That means, what are the day end, week end, month end and year end reports that every position is required to submit and to whom these reports are to be submitted. So, the final outcome of the chapters that define the organization structure aligned with the company goals, define roles of every position, define KRAs and then define the reporting from every position.

Now, a question must be there in the mind of the reader. Do I need to hire for every defined position defined in the organization structure? Answer is *NO!!* You may assign many positions to a single individual of the company, based on the number of transactions required for the current business scenario. Later, as business grows new hiring can be done to shift the roles based on the defined position.

One most important thing to note here is that none of the activities, advised in this chapter, should be done by keeping any individual person in mind. Once again, I am reiterating that keep people separate from the systems. For an organization the system is more important than who is handling it.

Chapter 4: Templates and Formats

Templates play a vital role in better functioning of any organization. We need to identify all kinds of documents whether for internal use or for external use and create a standard template for all. Using standard templates for all purposes has lot of advantages as:

1- It saves lots of time for the person creating a document as they have to simply put in the information / data at designated places and the documents are created.

2- The user of the document also knows the exact segment of the document where they have to look at to access the information and check the correctness of the documents.

3- Use of standard and nicely designed templates for the documents for the external parties creates a good impression about the company. Like a nicely designed and printed invoice leaves a good impression on the customers. Similarly, suppliers get a good impression from a great looking purchase order copy.

While designing the templates maximum information related to the company like contact details, all offices and branches, statutory details should be made an integral part of the templates. This creates a nice brand value and goodwill of the organization. It is generally observed that external templates like Order acknowledgement, Quotation, Invoice, Delivery Note, Purchase Order etc. are designed with all relevant information on it but when it comes to internal documents like Material Receipt Notes, Purchase Requisitions, Job Cards, Reimbursement Claim Forms etc designing is very casual and doesn't reflect seriousness. Internal documents should also be designed with all vital information on it. Often, statutory auditors who are external people get access to these documents. Therefore, any template whether for external purpose or internal purpose should be nicely designed and the positions handling/ using those documents should be carefully trained to use these templates.

Another very important aspect of creating templates is the numbering of it. Every template should have a provision of assigning a unique serial number to it. Serial numbering is very important for exercising control in the overall system. I have at times observed that only invoice numbering is maintained in the companies as this is the part of statutory requirement. For other templates often people do not use the numbering system. Without numbering any template the data capturing becomes almost impossible and at times organizations have no data for analysis and decision making.

Also the numbering should be done in a manner that the number of any document remains unique within the organization and just by looking at the number anyone is able to tell which template this number belongs to. There can be many methods to it and one may apply any mechanism of number defining with just two rules viz.

1. Any document being generated in the company whether for internal use or external use must carry a number and

2. The number assigned to any document is unique in nature.

Now once templates are designed and their numbering system is defined, we should create formats to record details of these templates in a summarized manner. We must create a format to record vital information (the variable part of the template) of every template. First two columns of such formats should be the document number and its date. Records should be maintained as per serial number and not as per date. Lower numbers should be recorded first and seriality order must be maintained.

In general, as per my observation, a very few organizations maintain such format for all the templates that they use. In fact this is magical. If we maintain data for all templates and documents, in a format, we will have an excellent database with us for future analysis, route cause tracing and strategy making. *This work wonders.*

Now, maintaining such format in a register, in an excel sheet, in a Google sheet or in an ERP/ Software is a separate matter of discussion which we will cover in chapter 7.

Chapter 5: Work Procedures

Work Procedures are nothing but the drilling down the defined processes. It's about the detailing of every process in a manner that any layman reading this document is able to perform the tasks. This is indeed a tedious task to define the work procedures for every task in the minutest manner, but it's the only way to get rid of manual dependency of any work. This will be a comprehensive document created for every position in the organization structure. Even the most complex and technical processes also can be written down in a manner that any layman is able to perform that task. Let's understand this with an example. One of the processes can be "Creating Invoice". This can be a part of the role of any particular position in the organization structure. Now, this becomes a specialized job and a person who has been making invoices previously is only supposed to do this. However, this can be done by any person if the following written *"Procedure of Creating Invoice"* is available in the training manual meant for that position.

"Procedure of Creating Invoice"

1- Open the blank invoice template.

2- Refer to the format where invoice data is captured and out the next invoice no.

3- Enter/ Write the Invoice no. in space below the *"Invoice No."* field in the template.

4- Enter today's date in the Date Field.

5- Open Customer's PO in front of you for reference.

6- In the *"Bill To"* field enter/ write the customer company's name, address & GST No. copying from customer's PO.

7- In the *"Ship To"* field enter the name, address and GST no as given in the customer's PO.

8- In the payment term field enter the same term as mentioned in the customer's PO.

9- Check the item details and quantities being shipped from the concerned team.

10- Write the product description same as mentioned in customer's PO.

11- Mention the quantity in the designated field in the template.

12- Copy the rate with currency from the customer's PO.

13- In the respective field mention the HSN code as mentioned in the customer's PO. In case HSN code is not mentioned in the customer's PO, consult the chartered accountant of the company or the competent person within the organization.

14- If the *Bill to* state is the same as our company's apply CGST & SGST in the designated field of the template else apply IGST.

15- Multiply the unit rate with the quantity and mention it in the Total column of the template.

16- For multiple items being shipped use separate line and mention the total in the column.

17- Do the total of the total column and mention in the designated field in the template.

18- Apply tax rate as per CGST & SGST/ IGST and mention the figure in the designated field. For tax rate consult the customer's PO or refer to the chartered accountant or competent authority in the company.

19- Mention the total in words in the designated field.

20- Due date of the payment to be calculated as per the payment terms and to be mentioned in the respective field.

21- Put company's round seal in the bottom of the invoice.

22- Get the Invoice signed from the Authorized Signatory.

Now by reading the above procedure anyone can prepare an invoice. We can create similar procedures for any process, activity or task. This will drastically reduce the dependency on manpower for any work/ position in the organization.

Procedure of everything is defined in the same fashion, in companies like McDonalds where nothing is dependent on people.

Another great advantage of defining procedures is that there are least chances of errors. Work happens so mechanically that it is faster and least prone to errors.

Chapter 6: Control Mechanism

Indian mythological book *Ram Charit Manas* says *"Bhaya Bin Hoye Na Preet"* means there is no performance without fear. Best of the performances and results come from the fear and pressure. This applies for the performances in the business operations as well.

While designing the systems and processes of the organization, various kinds of control mechanisms need to be applied. In chapter 4 we have talked about defining the unique numbering systems for every document being used in the company. This is nothing but a control mechanism. By serializing any document it becomes extremely easy to control, track and compile the details very easily.

I recently came across a company which has been in business for the last 22 years and they do not record their quotations with serial numbering. This results in missing out lots and lots of orders as whosoever submits a quotation against any enquiry keeps the information to their level only, due to which most of the times there is no follow up on quotations. Company is doing satisfactory business and the promoter is happy with their performance without any realization that they have potential and can increase their business multifold, just by exercising the control mechanism on their quotation management process. It's not the story of only this company, but of almost every traditional family run family owned SMEs.

Before we proceed further, I would like to discuss the need of exercising the control mechanism in the organization. In fact it's psychological that the human mind is lazy in nature. It needs a push to remain active. And this push comes from two things, one is burning desire and other is fear. Only these two factors drive the human mind to perform. Driven by the burning desires are the entrepreneurs who perform to achieve something in their lives. However, it's a bitter truth that 95+% of employed work force perform only under fear or pressure. We can co-relate this with our own organizations. Our workforce often becomes complacent, if they are not being watched. That's the reason; we will see that even most of the offices, CCTV cameras are installed. This is also one kind of control mechanism. Though, I do not advocate CCTV cameras being a control mechanism.

The fact is that *MONEY* is the best control mechanism in the businesses. Performance comes best only when work is associated with monetary incentive or punishment. One of the next examples is the incentive plans for the sales team. Companies spend a lot of time and energy in designing the incentive plans for the sales team. And this works also, very well. This is so lucrative that I have seen so many sales professionals who earn double, triple of their salaries as incentive only. However, it is quite a challenging task and companies keep struggling to design incentive plans for the non sales functions in the organizations as defining measurable and monitoring becomes such a tedious task in SMEs that it always remains in planning and designing end only and never comes to the stage of implementation.

Rewards and punishments are the best control mechanisms in any organization. Companies need to find out the innovative ways to implement rewards and punishments to ensure the best of the efficiencies and results in the organization. In chapter 3 we have learnt to define the KRA for every position in the organization but we need to what KRAs have achieved or not achieved. To ensure the accomplishment of the KRAs, it needs to be linked with rewards and punishments.

I find a very innovative way of this in the organization where I do my consulting. They have a system of day end reporting by every team member as how have they spent their entire day. Every team member is supposed to report the work that they have done during different time slots of the day. This system was not effective until the punishment mechanism came in picture. Almost 50% of the staff used to **"FORGET"** to report or many had developed a habit of submitting a combined report of 2-3 days together. The business owner one fine morning announced that whosoever does not submit their day end report will have to mandatorily deposit Rs. 100.00 next morning to the accountant in cash. Such collected cash was again used for employee welfare only. This worked and no one forgets to submit their day end report. Success rate is now more than 95%.

Similarly I have seen many companies, controlling the late coming habits of their staff by imposing the monetary penalties. Another company I know, where the sales team had a habit of submitting the 3-4 months combined conveyance claims. This was having a big impact on the monthly MISs and management was never able to see the accurate monthly profitability figures. They implemented a system that, if a salesperson does not submit its monthly reimbursement claim by end of the month, it will never be approved and paid. Within 2 months after a few rejections all claims were being submitted on time.

"Money" is the best control mechanism. Therefore all processes in the organization would be linked to money in some manner or other.

KRAs of every position to be made measurable and with that the annual increments can be linked to ensure best of the performances of the individual member of the team. Another control mechanism is the review meetings. There should be a schedule of daily/ weekly review meetings of all departments and should be rigorously followed. This should be an agenda based meeting with a proper checklist of points of discussions and attendance in this meeting must be must for all. The entire pattern, agenda, timelines, attendees should be pre-defined. Action points and Minutes of Meetings should be well recorded and circulated among attendees then and there only. It is observed that often companies have the mechanism of meeting but MOM circulation happens very late and by that time some of the action points lose their sanctity.

Generally, meetings are called arbitrarily and in case of arising of any problem only. There should be a well-defined method of calling SOS meetings also. However, if these are pre-defined schedules and agenda of meetings, chances of SOS meetings will be very less.

To summarize this, there should be separate documents created, mentioning the meetings, agenda, the chairperson and MOM recording person of these meetings, for the entire year. I have not seen a SME yet in my career so far which rigorously creates such a calendar, but I firmly believe that if this document is created, the need of SOS meetings shall be minimized to a greater extent. SOS meetings are one of the biggest time killers in the organizations.

The last control mechanism that I wish to explain is the record keeping mechanism. Often it is observed that people spent a lot of their valuable times in tracing the historic documents. There can be a lot of innovative ways that every single company can find for record keeping. But going by my experience so far working on system and processes, here are the suggested ways of record keeping:

- Separate files/ folders to be created for master documents of the company.
- Like a file/ folder for all the registration documents
- Creating a separate file/ folder for every single sales order coming in the company. All documents pertaining to any order must be stored in respective file/ folder.

- Separate file for all document types by maintaining its serial in order.

If we follow only above three, we can create a robust filing mechanism in the company.

To summarize till now, following 5 mechanisms can exercise best of the controls over the entire system:

1- Serial Numbering

2- Rewards and Punishments

3- End point of every process is linked with money

4- Review Meetings and

5- Record Keeping

Chapter 7: Systems and Processes Vs Automation

Let's go back to the era, 25 years from today when computers were not there but systems were still there. Businesses, government works, schools, colleges, hospitals or anything were having the manual systems for everything. Print formats were being used in booklet form, registers were being used for record keeping, and physical filing mechanism, control system through note sheets etc. were in practice. All these things have been replaced with software, cloud storage, soft copy of documents etc. But the fact remains that these automation has happened in the systems in practice and it's not the replacement of the systems.

I often come across a situation when system and process discussion turns to automation discussion, while both are separate subjects. When we talk about automation, it is replacement of manpower in some manner and not of the systems and processes. For any kind of automation first desired result is refined, then systems to achieve those results are made and then that system is mapped in software supported by hardware to automate the system. Automation has immense benefit in terms of efficiency and exercising control mechanisms. Removal of chances of error in any work is also one of the biggest advantages of automation.

Automation of business systems and processes are one of the major challenges of the SMEs. This is merely because of lack of understanding the correct process of automation. At times, a SME entrepreneur assumes that company selling software to them will take care of their systems and processes. In fact while selling software, IT companies explain the features available in their software but at the time of implementation proper mapping of the company's existing systems is not done in the software.

If we search the success ratio of ERP implementation in SMEs, on Google, we will find a shocking result that more than 70% ERP implementations in SMEs are termed as failed. I myself have come across so many SME entrepreneurs who had already formed a wrong opinion against a particular make of ERP. They have declared that software as the worst software, whereas fact is something else. No ERP or software is bad. Any software company creates an ERP or industry specific / task specific software after lots of study and research. The software, per say, are not wrong, but their implementation is. The basic reason for such implementation failures is lack of correct mediation of an expert who has thorough understanding of business processes and also understands the ERP/ Software structure in totality. While deciding to go for automation, a dedicated person from within the organization or outside organization should be assigned the task of implementation of any automation tool whether it's CRM/ ERP or any other software. It is extremely important that during the phase of implementation, this position's role should only be the automation. This resource should have a thorough understanding of all functions within the organization including marketing, sales, operations, inventory, purchase, export, import, accounts, finance, logistics, HR, production, PPC, maintenance etc.

The first activity of starting automation implementation should be to re-engineer the entire systems and processes within the company. Then it should be to identify the correct software due diligence from all available options in the marketplace. One important aspect of software implementation is the decision making on server selection. Indian SME owners, in general, are very obsessed about their data security and often refute to believe that the cloud server providers are at times more safe than the in-house servers. In today's scenario deciding to go for an in-house server is not a wise decision. It's not cost effective in terms of acquisition, maintenance, keeping it online 24 X 7, technology and software upgradations etc. Cloud servers are the viable option in today's scenario. Moreover, implementing the SAAS (Software as Service) based software are even more viable option than maintaining a cloud based server. This gives more flexibility in terms of shifting from one software to another without any hassle. Having SAAS based software also saves the initial capital cost incurred in operating software and databases.

However, the decision of infrastructure is an individual's understanding and one should take enough advice before deciding on the same. It is highly recommended to not to stick to the stigma of safety of data and information. These, in my opinion, are more prone to be stolen from the in-house servers than the cloud servers or from the SAAS based software, This is strictly my own opinion and one should not make decisions under the influence of my opinion.

Coming back to systems and processes, the implementer has to first understand the software well which he/ she is going to implement. Understanding functionality and features of this is of utmost important part. Now the blueprint of mapping the company's systems and processes in the software should be prepared. Generally this task is done by the functional consultants of the software company, who most of the time are technical experts and have less understanding of the business processes and functions. This part of the implementation should be out of the scope of the software company. They should be involved just for the mapping part as per the advice of this dedicated resource. This will decrease the costing of the software company and they will be able to offer better discounts on their initial offers.

If the blueprint preparation part is done with focus, implementation of the software is bound to be successful. Another important part of implementing any software is the user training. Once mapping is done.

Training should be done by this resource only as he/ she understands the language of both sides i.e. of the user side as well as of the software side.If the implementation is done properly using above methodology, keeping documentation of subjects explained in chapter 5 & chapter 6 may not be required as those can be easily mapped in the software being implemented. Automation of the systems can be done to any level. The more automation company will do the requirement of the manpower that too skilled and experienced manpower will keep reducing. Ideally one should not decide to go for the complete automation in one go. Automation in the first phase can be done to the level up to the software as the ready product (without any alteration or customization) can handle. Later forward or backward integration using customized tools or other software should be done to bring in more and more efficiency and control in the overall system. It's a continuous process. Need for further automation could be identified with the increase in number of transactions and with the increasing workload of the users. Here, I would like to add an example for better understanding. This comes from my experience with one of my oldest clients. We had implemented one of the renowned ERP in the company with only two user licenses. One fine day I got a call from one of the users of the ERP saying that workload has increased and we need to attach one more staff with that user. Without recommending a new hiring to the management, I spent one half day with that ERP user. I noticed that his major time goes in attending the calls of the sales team of the company spread across India, asking for the availability of stock and its landed cost. I found an automation solution to it. With the help of the ERP's technical expert, we created excel based report which fetches the data on a real time basis from the database of the ERP directly. Now this excel report of inventory was circulated to the entire sales team throughout India. They saved this report on their desktops and had a real time status of inventory and its landed cost without calling this centralized ERP user. This vanished the requirement of a new hiring immediately as that ERP user saved his almost half day which he used to spend in answering the calls.

Using above methodology, continuous improvement and efficiency building can be done through automation in any organization. All you need to have is that person who monitors the need of it and its one, either internal or external.

I often face a question from my SME friends as to which ERP/ CRM/ Software is the best. To answer that I always say that, if implemented well, any ERP/ CRM is the best. No software is bad, only its improper implementation makes it bad. For that matter today G Suite from Google is also becoming very popular among SMEs as its SAAS based software and very much affordable in terms of prices. Its ease of accessibility is making it extremely popular these days. However, only learning G Suite will not help, its proper implementation by a functional expert can only give best results from it.

To summarize this chapter, I would once again repeat that systems and processes are entirely different from automation. First systems and processes should be well worked on and then automation should be done for increasing efficiency of those systems and processes. And if the automation part is well handled and continuously improved, there comes a time when organization would not need the middle management positions at all. Only top management and lower management can run the entire show with ease.

Chapter 8: Building a Team

Though I do not consider myself an expert of the subject but I am covering this in my book, as this is an important aspect of business growth. A great team is also of the same importance as the systems and processes.

From previous chapters readers would have got some negative impressions about having a great team. Let's not get biased. A great team and systems go parallel to take the organization to the newer heights. While building the team, refer to the organization structure that you have prepared. You need to have people fitting in those positions. Hiring should be done by matching the roles and the KRAs defined for the position.

One most important thing that I would like to share here from my experience so far is that people must be hired for their attitude and aptitude. Keep knowledge, experience and credentials secondary while making judgment for a prospective team. A person with the wrong attitude can do a lot of damage to your growth plan, no matter how knowledgeable and experienced he / she is. At the same time a person with a right and positive attitude will work towards attaining those knowledge and expertise which is required to achieve the organization goals. A wrong attitude person will always keep cribbing about what the company is doing for him/ her while a right attitude person will first see what he / she can do for the company. There is a lot that can be said about the attitude but since this is not the topic of this book, I am leaving it here. Readers may refer to many renowned books available on attitude.

Second is aptitude. A person with high aptitude should be preferred always while selecting the team. It does not matter if he/ she has the required set of knowledge and experience because a person with high aptitude will take no time to learn the required set of skills and knowledge. Again this is a vast subject and can be learnt from the many books that are available on the subject.

Besides looking for two must required traits that are attitude and aptitude, temperament of the prospective team shall also be judged carefully. Though it's difficult to find out that, selecting the team as even the most short tempered person keeps good cool while representing for the employment.

So while hiring check for:

- Attitude
- Aptitude
- Alignment with the position in the organization
- Cool Temperament

We all would have heard or even experienced many people who joined some organization as office boys or clerks but with time attained the highest positions in the organizations. There are so many stories like this. These are the right attitude and aptitude people.

An entrepreneur should not be dependent on the traditional ways of hiring, but should remain vigilant always while meeting people during networking events, social events, travelling etc. A great teammate can be hired from anywhere.

Now, the team is hired, take good care of them. Once again this is a vast topic and can be learnt from elsewhere but must be learnt.

If you are good to the team, you are half done of the work. Many entrepreneurs have developed a belief that shouting and screaming brings best results. Actually this belief comes because they have the wrong attitude towards people in the team. If you need to shout on a team member to get the work done most of the time, replace them without any hesitation because as an entrepreneur you are not supposed to lose your cool.

Be empathetic to the team's personal needs. Taking care of their physical and mental comfort can result in a great team building.

Now while talking above, I would like you to understand that you have not to fall in love with the team. So take good care of the team but do not fall in love with them. Any teammate which is hindrance in achieving the organizational goals must be removed from the position. I have seen numerous occasions in Indian SME scenarios that the entrepreneur is so emotional that they tend to harm the company's goals in order to please a particular person for one reason or another. To such people I advise that, if you are in love with an employee, please take care of them in personal capacity but do not burden the company with non profitable assets. We all know the basics of business, that businessman is different from business. So:

- Select the right team
- Take good care of them
- But do not fall in love with them

Chapter 9: Focus on Marketing & Sales

An entrepreneur's only job is marketing of their products or services, not even the sales. No one can do better marketing of any organization other than the promoter. But the irony is that they lose focus from this very activity and remain involved with the operations. At times, they are seen to be dreaming (they call it goal) to multiply their business manifold but are so engrossed in the operations that they refute to understand the importance of systems and process while this is the only way that they can free themselves to focus only on marketing activities.The position of Marketing Head/ Sales Head should be occupied only by the promoter and more than 80-90 % focus should be given for that position only. Not more than 10-20% time has to be devoted for all other functions defined in the organization chart. Moreover, the entire marketing and Sales team should also be working under strong systems. There should be a strong control mechanism for this team as well. Marketing & Sales team being the front face of the organization should be controlled well on what they offer and commit to the market. Their offers and commitments should be well aligned to the company goals. I would not talk in detail about the deliverables of this team as there are a lot available on the subject. The Marketing and Sales team should not have a permanent seating space in the company premise. Often I have seen that this team is involved in all company activities and operations but sales. In one of my consulting assignments, we decided to not allow the sales team to come to office but to report directly in the market 5 days in a week. We did some changes in the systems and automated some processes so that the need of this team coming to office was not there anymore. This resulted in a 10% increase in the organization's new clientele in just one month time.

When the entire operations of the company is running on systems and processes and the promoter spends 80-90% of his/ her time only on Marketing and Sales activities, business is bound to grow manifold. There will be a mathematical outcome to the results. Try this to believe this.

NOW

RUN your business on *AUTOPILOT*

and

KEEP GROWING

With Best Wishes...........

Shailendra Chaurasia

॥ इति॥

www.ingramcontent.com/pod-product-compliance
Lightning Source LLC
Chambersburg PA
CBHW030546220526
45463CB00007B/2995